Mastering TikTok: A Guide to Creating Viral Videos

Table of Contents:

Introduction
- Understanding the TikTok Algorithm
- The Power of Virality

Chapter 1: Finding Your Niche
- 1.1 Identifying Your Passion
- 1.2 Researching Trending Niches on TikTok

Chapter 2: Crafting Captivating Content
- 2.1 Storytelling Techniques
- 2.2 Utilizing Music and Sound Effects
- 2.3 Incorporating Humor and Trends

Chapter 3: Optimizing Your Profile
- 3.1 Creating an Eye-Catching Profile Picture
- 3.2 Crafting an Engaging Bio
- 3.3 Linking Other Social Media Profiles

Chapter 4: Leveraging TikTok Features
- 4.1 Exploring Filters and Effects
- 4.2 Using Duet and Stitch Features
- 4.3 Understanding Challenges and Hashtags

Chapter 5: Consistency and Timing
- 5.1 Establishing a Posting Schedule
- 5.2 Analyzing Peak Engagement Times

Chapter 6: Engaging with the TikTok Community
- 6.1 Responding to Comments and Messages
- 6.2 Collaborating with Other TikTok Creators
- 6.3 Participating in Challenges

Chapter 7: Analyzing Analytics
- 7.1 Understanding TikTok Analytics
- 7.2 Adjusting Strategies Based on Data

Chapter 8: Going Beyond Virality
- 8.1 Monetization Strategies
- 8.2 Building a Brand on TikTok

Conclusion
- Recap of Key Strategies
  - Looking Ahead to Future Trends
  -

BONUS TOOLS

Unleashing Creativity with CapCut

Welcome to the dynamic world of TikTok, where creativity knows no bounds and trends evolve at the speed of a well-executed dance move. In "Mastering TikTok: A Guide to Creating Viral Videos," we embark on an exciting journey into the heart of one of the most influential social media platforms of our time.

In an era where content reigns supreme, TikTok has emerged as a cultural phenomenon, providing a stage for individuals from all walks of life to showcase their talent, humor, and unique perspectives. Whether you're an aspiring content creator, a business looking to leverage the power of social media, or simply a curious observer, this book is your passport to unlocking the secrets of TikTok success.

From navigating the platform's features to deciphering the latest trends, "Mastering TikTok" is your comprehensive roadmap to not only understanding the mechanics of the app but also mastering the art of creating content that resonates with a global audience. With its short-form videos, catchy challenges, and diverse array of content, TikTok has become a breeding ground for creativity and a launchpad for viral sensations.

Throughout the pages of this guide, we'll delve into the strategies and techniques employed by TikTok's most successful creators. From crafting engaging narratives to harnessing the power of music and dance, each chapter is designed to equip you with the tools you need to stand out in the crowded TikTok landscape.

Prepare to unravel the mysteries behind trending hashtags, discover the psychology of virality, and gain insights into the ever-evolving algorithms that shape the content we consume. Whether you're aiming to entertain, educate, or inspire, "Mastering TikTok" will empower you to leverage the full potential of this dynamic platform and elevate your content to new heights.

So, whether you're a seasoned TikTok enthusiast or a newcomer eager to make your mark, join us on this exhilarating adventure as we navigate the exhilarating world of TikTok and uncover the keys to creating videos that captivate and resonate in the digital age. The stage is set, the spotlight is on – let the TikTok mastery begin!

"Understanding the TikTok Algorithm":

In the ever-evolving landscape of social media, where attention spans are fleeting, and trends come and go in the blink of an eye, understanding the algorithms that govern content visibility is the key to unlocking success. Nowhere is this truer than on TikTok, a platform that has revolutionized the way we consume and create content.

"Mastering TikTok: A Guide to Creating Viral Videos" takes you deep into the heartbeat of TikTok's success—its algorithm. In this chapter, we unravel the intricacies of the algorithm that propels content from obscurity to the coveted realm of virality. Behind the mesmerizing dance challenges, comedic skits, and diverse content lies a sophisticated system that determines what captures the audience's attention.

As we embark on the journey of understanding the TikTok algorithm, we will demystify the factors that contribute to the visibility of your videos. From the importance of engagement metrics to the nuances of the For You Page (FYP), we'll navigate the algorithmic landscape that shapes the fate of every TikTok creator.

Throughout these pages, you'll gain insights into the algorithm's machine learning capabilities, exploring how it adapts to user preferences and refines its understanding of what constitutes engaging content. The algorithmic dance between creators and the platform is a dynamic one, and this guide aims to equip you with the knowledge and strategies to choreograph your content for success.

Whether you're aiming for a single moment in the viral spotlight or seeking sustained growth, "Understanding the TikTok Algorithm" is your compass through the digital wilderness. Join us as we delve into the algorithms that determine the fate of videos, explore the impact of trends on visibility, and uncover the tips and tricks that can elevate your content above the digital noise.

As we navigate the algorithmic currents of TikTok, prepare to not only comprehend the science behind viral content but also to leverage this knowledge to amplify your voice and captivate audiences in the vast and vibrant TikTok community. Let the journey into the heart of the TikTok algorithm begin!

"Understanding the TikTok Algorithm" from "Mastering TikTok: A Guide to Creating Viral Videos":

Welcome to the digital realm where short-form videos reign supreme, creativity flourishes, and trends take flight at the speed of a double-tap. In the captivating journey of "Mastering TikTok: A Guide to Creating Viral Videos," we now venture into the beating heart of TikTok's success—the elusive yet powerful TikTok algorithm.

In an era where content creation has become an art form, and social media platforms serve as stages for expression, the TikTok algorithm is the invisible force that shapes the destiny of each video that graces the platform. This chapter is your backstage pass, your behind-the-scenes glimpse into the intricate workings of the algorithm that determines what captures the attention of millions.

Understanding the TikTok algorithm isn't just about decoding a set of rules; it's about unraveling the digital tapestry that connects creators with their audience. As we embark on this exploration, we'll navigate the algorithmic landscape that decides which videos make it to the For You Page (FYP), TikTok's holy grail of content discovery.

This guide is your compass through the algorithmic wilderness, providing insights into the factors that influence content visibility, the metrics that matter, and the dance between creators and the algorithm itself. From the role of engagement to the impact of trends, we'll uncover the secrets that can turn a video from a mere upload to a viral sensation.

Join us on this journey of discovery as we delve into the inner workings of the TikTok algorithm, unravel its mysteries, and equip you with the knowledge to strategically navigate its currents. Whether you're a seasoned creator aiming for the next big hit or a newcomer looking to make your mark, "Understanding the TikTok Algorithm" is your guide to mastering the algorithmic dance that defines success on TikTok. Let's dive in and decode the algorithmic magic that transforms videos into digital sensations.

Chapter 1: "Finding Your Niche" from "Mastering TikTok: A Guide to Creating Viral Videos":

In the vibrant tapestry of TikTok, where creativity knows no bounds and trends evolve with a rhythm of their own, finding your niche is the first step on the exhilarating journey to mastering the art of viral videos. Welcome to Chapter 1 of "Mastering TikTok: A Guide to Creating Viral Videos" where we embark on a quest to discover the unique corner of this dynamic platform where your creativity can shine.

In the vast and diverse landscape of TikTok, where millions of users scroll, dance, and share their stories, identifying your niche is akin to claiming your space on the digital stage. This chapter is your compass, guiding you through the process of self-discovery and helping you carve out a niche that aligns with your passions, talents, and the interests of your potential audience.

As we delve into the intricacies of finding your niche, we'll explore the importance of authenticity in a space defined by its diversity. From the world of makeup tutorials to comedic sketches, dance challenges to educational content, TikTok offers a canvas for every shade of creativity. Discovering your niche isn't just about standing out; it's about resonating with a community that shares your enthusiasm.

Throughout these pages, we'll navigate the terrain of trending content, explore the power of storytelling, and provide you with the tools to identify the sweet spot where your passion intersects with audience demand. Whether you're a budding artist, a knowledgeable expert, or a storyteller at heart, this chapter will empower you to not only find your niche but to leverage it for TikTok success.

So, let the exploration begin. Join us as we unravel the secrets of discovering your niche on TikTok, a journey that sets the stage for your unique voice to echo through the digital corridors of this vibrant platform. Chapter 1 is your gateway to a personalized TikTok experience, where your creativity takes center stage, and your journey to viral success begins.

1.1 Identifying Your Passion

In the kaleidoscope of TikTok's vast and diverse content, your journey to mastering the platform begins with a crucial step—identifying your passion. This chapter is not just about standing out; it's about discovering the essence of what makes you tick, what makes your creative spirit dance, and what sets your content apart in the dynamic world of TikTok.

Embracing Authenticity

Before you dive into the realm of viral videos and trending challenges, take a moment to reflect on what truly inspires you. Authenticity is the linchpin of success on TikTok, and it begins with embracing your genuine interests. Whether you're a makeup enthusiast, a fitness aficionado, a tech whiz, or a storyteller, your authenticity becomes the magnetic force that attracts like-minded individuals to your content.

The Power of Personal Connection

Identifying your passion isn't just a strategic move; it's the foundation for building a personal connection with your audience. In this digital age, users gravitate towards content that feels real, relatable, and sincere. As you explore your passions, consider how they align with the interests and desires of your potential audience. This alignment is the key to creating a community around your content.

Navigating the Vast Landscape

TikTok is a treasure trove of diverse niches, each with its own audience and trends. As you embark on the journey of identifying your passion, explore the myriad of content categories on the platform. From beauty and fashion to science and education, there's a niche for every interest. Your challenge is to find the intersection where your passion meets the needs and curiosities of your target audience.

Exercises for Self-Discovery

To kickstart the process of identifying your passion, consider engaging in self-discovery exercises. Reflect on your hobbies, interests, and the topics that light a spark within you. Ask yourself: What are the subjects that I could talk about for hours on end? What skills do I possess that I can showcase on TikTok? By answering these questions, you'll uncover the threads that will weave into the fabric of your unique niche.

As you navigate the landscape of identifying your passion, remember that TikTok is not just a platform; it's a community waiting to embrace the authenticity and uniqueness that only you can bring. In the upcoming sections of this chapter, we'll delve deeper into refining your niche, aligning it with trends, and strategically positioning yourself for TikTok success. Get ready to turn your passion into a powerful force on the TikTok stage.

1.2 Researching Trending Niches on TikTok

In the ever-evolving landscape of TikTok, staying attuned to trending niches is a strategic move that can propel your content from the shadows to the spotlight. As we continue our journey in "Mastering TikTok: A Guide to Creating Viral Videos," this section of Chapter 1 is dedicated to the art of researching and identifying niches that not only align with your passion but also resonate with the pulse of the TikTok community.

The Dynamic Nature of TikTok Trends

TikTok is a platform that thrives on trends. From dance challenges to viral hashtags, the landscape is in constant flux as users engage with and amplify the latest trends. To find your niche, it's crucial to observe and understand the dynamic nature of TikTok trends. What's capturing the audience's attention today might evolve tomorrow, and being adaptable is key to staying relevant.

Exploring the Discover Page

The Discover Page, a gateway to trending content on TikTok, is a goldmine for identifying popular niches. Spend time scrolling through this section to observe the types of videos that are gaining traction. Note the common themes, styles, and tones that resonate with the audience. This exploration will not only inspire your content creation but also provide valuable insights into the diverse niches thriving on TikTok.

Engaging with TikTok Challenges

Challenges are the lifeblood of TikTok trends. Participating in or even just observing popular challenges can offer a glimpse into the niches capturing the collective imagination of users. Keep an eye on challenges related to your interests, and consider how you can infuse your unique perspective into these trends. It's a powerful way to ride the wave of existing trends while injecting your own creativity.

Leveraging Hashtags for Insight

Hashtags are more than just labels; they are gateways to entire communities on TikTok. By exploring trending and popular hashtags related to your interests, you can unearth hidden niches and discover content creators who are thriving in those spaces. This hashtag research not only helps you identify trending topics but also provides an avenue to connect with like-minded creators and potential collaborators.

Navigating the FYP Algorithm

Understanding the For You Page (FYP) algorithm is essential in researching trending niches. The FYP serves as a personalized feed of content based on user preferences and engagement. By observing the content that surfaces on your FYP, you gain insights into the niches and trends tailored to your interests. It's a curated window into the ever-shifting landscape of TikTok content.

As you embark on the journey of researching trending niches, remember that this is not about conforming to existing trends but about finding your unique intersection within them. This chapter lays the foundation for discovering where your passion aligns with the dynamic trends of TikTok. In the subsequent sections, we will delve deeper into refining your niche, strategizing your content, and positioning yourself for TikTok success. Get ready to not only follow trends but to shape and influence them with your creative voice.

Chapter 2: Crafting Captivating Content

Welcome to Chapter 2 of "Mastering TikTok: A Guide to Creating Viral Videos." In the ever-evolving landscape of social media, TikTok has emerged as a powerhouse, providing creators with a platform to showcase their creativity, share stories, and captivate audiences worldwide. As we delve into the heart of this guide, we recognize that mastering TikTok isn't just about understanding the technicalities; it's about weaving a narrative that resonates with your audience.

Chapter 2, titled "Crafting Captivating Content," is your gateway to the art of storytelling in the TikTok realm. Here, we will unravel the secrets behind videos that not only grab attention but leave a lasting impact. Crafting content for TikTok involves a delicate balance of creativity, authenticity, and an acute awareness of your audience's preferences. Whether you're a seasoned creator or just embarking on your TikTok journey, this chapter will equip you with the tools and insights to elevate your content creation game.

In the following pages, we'll explore the anatomy of viral videos, dissecting the elements that contribute to their success. From understanding TikTok trends to harnessing the power of storytelling, we'll guide you through a step-by-step process to help you conceptualize, script, and produce videos that stand out in the crowded TikTok landscape.

Get ready to discover the principles that turn ordinary videos into memorable experiences. As we embark on this journey through Chapter 2, be prepared to unleash your creativity, experiment with new ideas, and gain the skills needed to craft content that not only entertains but leaves a lasting impression on the ever-scrolling minds of TikTok users. Let's dive into the art of crafting captivating content and make your mark in the TikTok universe.

2.1 Storytelling Techniques

Welcome to the heart of "Mastering TikTok: A Guide to Creating Viral Videos," where we dive deep into the art of crafting captivating content. In this chapter, we explore the power of storytelling on TikTok—an essential skill that transforms mere videos into compelling narratives that resonate with audiences worldwide.

The Narrative Arc in 60 Seconds

TikTok's unique challenge lies in its short-form nature, where creators have a mere 60 seconds to captivate and engage their audience. Effective storytelling in this brief timeframe requires a keen understanding of the narrative arc. Begin with a hook that grabs attention within the first few seconds, escalate the tension or interest, and conclude with a satisfying resolution or call to action. Mastering this condensed narrative structure is the key to holding the viewer's attention from start to finish.

Personalizing Your Story

One of TikTok's strengths is its emphasis on authenticity and personal connection. Successful creators often weave their own stories into their content, allowing viewers to glimpse the person behind the screen. Whether sharing personal experiences, anecdotes, or moments from your life, infusing authenticity into your content creates a relatable connection with your audience. Remember, authenticity is magnetic, and viewers are drawn to content that feels genuine.

Utilizing Visual Storytelling

On TikTok, storytelling extends beyond words. Visual elements play a crucial role in conveying emotions, ideas, and narratives. Leverage the platform's creative features—visual effects, transitions, and text overlays—to enhance your storytelling. Consider the use of dynamic camera angles and creative editing techniques to add layers to your narrative. The combination of compelling visuals and a well-crafted story is a recipe for TikTok success.

Engaging Emotions

Emotions are the currency of storytelling. Whether it's humor, joy, surprise, or empathy, tapping into emotions resonates deeply with viewers. Craft your content to evoke emotional responses, drawing your audience into a shared experience. Emotionally charged content is more likely to be shared and remembered, contributing to the potential for virality on TikTok.

Embracing TikTok Trends in Storytelling

TikTok is a platform driven by trends, and storytelling is no exception. Pay attention to the storytelling techniques that align with popular trends on the platform. From duet challenges to lip-syncing trends, incorporating these elements into your narrative can amplify your content's visibility and engagement.

As you navigate the realm of storytelling on TikTok, remember that each video is an opportunity to connect, entertain, and leave a lasting impression. In the upcoming sections of this chapter, we will delve into refining your storytelling techniques, exploring diverse content styles, and understanding the impact of creativity on virality. Prepare to elevate your content creation skills as we unravel the secrets of crafting narratives that resonate in the fast-paced world of TikTok.

2.2 Utilizing Music and Sound Effects

In the symphony of short-form videos that is TikTok, the strategic use of music and sound effects is the secret sauce that elevates content from mundane to memorable. Welcome to Chapter 2 of "Mastering TikTok: A Guide to Creating Viral Videos," where we explore the art of harmonizing your visual storytelling with the auditory magic of music and sound.

The Rhythmic Pulse of TikTok

Music is the heartbeat of TikTok, and creators harness its power to enhance storytelling, set the tone, and create a memorable viewing experience. TikTok's extensive music library offers a vast array of genres, moods, and beats to suit any content style. Whether it's a catchy tune for a dance challenge or a poignant melody for emotional storytelling, choosing the right soundtrack is a strategic decision that can significantly impact audience engagement.

Riding the Wave of TikTok Trends

TikTok's music trends often transcend the audio realm and become integral components of viral challenges and memes. Keeping a keen eye (or ear) on the latest musical trends on the platform allows you to stay ahead of the curve. Participating in or incorporating trending songs into your content not only aligns your videos with popular challenges but also increases the likelihood of your content being discovered on the For You Page.

Crafting Atmosphere with Sound Effects

Beyond music, sound effects are invaluable tools for crafting atmosphere and enhancing the impact of your content. Whether it's the subtle rustling of leaves, the roar of applause, or the comedic sound bite that punctuates a punchline, sound effects add layers to your storytelling. TikTok's sound library includes a plethora of effects to choose from, allowing you to tailor the auditory experience to complement your narrative.

The Choreography of Dance and Music

For dance challenges, the relationship between choreography and music is a dance of its own. Crafting engaging dance content involves not only mastering the moves but also synchronizing them with the rhythm and beats of the chosen music. The seamless integration of dance and music is a powerful combination that captures the viewer's attention and makes your content stand out on the crowded TikTok stage.

Leveraging Original Sounds

Originality is a cornerstone of TikTok success, and creating or using unique sounds can set your content apart. Whether it's composing an original track, recording your voice, or using an unconventional sound bite, original sounds contribute to the distinctive identity of your videos. Originality not only attracts viewers but also encourages them to engage and share, a key factor in the journey to virality.

As we conclude our exploration of utilizing music and sound effects on TikTok, remember that the auditory dimension is as crucial as the visual in the world of short-form videos. In the upcoming sections of this chapter, we'll delve into refining your content creation skills, exploring additional creative elements, and understanding the nuances of engagement. Get ready to orchestrate a symphony of sights and sounds that captivates your audience and propels your TikTok journey to new heights.

2.3 Incorporating Humor and Trends

Welcome to the laughter-filled, ever-evolving landscape of TikTok, where humor and trends reign supreme. In this section of "Mastering TikTok: A Guide to Creating Viral Videos," we delve into the art of infusing humor into your content and riding the wave of trending challenges, making your videos not just entertaining but irresistibly shareable.

The Power of TikTok Humor

Humor is the universal language of TikTok, transcending cultures and languages to bring joy to millions of viewers worldwide. Whether your style is witty one-liners, slapstick comedy, or clever satire, incorporating humor into your content is a surefire way to capture attention. TikTok's algorithm favors content that elicits positive reactions, making humor a strategic tool for engagement.

Crafting Viral Comedy

Creating viral comedy on TikTok involves more than just telling jokes. It's about understanding the platform's unique comedic styles, leveraging trends, and showcasing your authentic sense of humor. Observing popular comedians on TikTok, analyzing successful skits, and experimenting with your comedic style can help you discover what resonates with your audience.

Riding the Trending Wave

TikTok's heartbeat is the rhythm of trends, and aligning your content with popular challenges and memes is a potent strategy for visibility. Trending challenges provide a framework for creativity, allowing you to put your unique spin on popular concepts. Participating in these trends not only keeps your content relevant but also exposes it to a broader audience through the algorithm's affinity for trending topics.

Putting a Twist on Trends

While jumping on trends is essential, putting your unique twist on them is the key to standing out. Whether it's a dance challenge, lip-sync trend, or a viral hashtag, consider how you can infuse your personality and creativity into the trend. Adding an unexpected element or incorporating humor into trending challenges can elevate your content and make it memorable.

Balancing Consistency and Creativity

While trends are a powerful tool, striking a balance between participating in popular challenges and creating original content is crucial. Consistency in participating in trends builds visibility, but injecting your creativity and unique perspective ensures that your content doesn't get lost in the crowd. The magic lies in the dance between riding trends and showcasing your individuality.

As we conclude our exploration of incorporating humor and trends on TikTok, remember that laughter and cultural resonance are potent forces in the world of short-form videos. In the upcoming sections of this chapter, we'll continue to refine your content creation skills, exploring additional creative elements, and understanding the nuances of audience engagement. Get ready to infuse your videos with humor, ride the trends, and master the art of crafting content that captivates the TikTok community.

Chapter 3: Optimizing Your Profile

Welcome to Chapter 3 of "Mastering TikTok: A Guide to Creating Viral Videos." Now that we've explored the foundations of crafting compelling content in Chapter 2, we turn our attention to a crucial aspect of your TikTok journey — your profile. In this digital realm where first impressions are formed in a matter of seconds, optimizing your profile is the key to unlocking the full potential of your TikTok presence.

Titled "Optimizing Your Profile," this chapter serves as your roadmap to creating an inviting and engaging TikTok persona. Your profile is more than just a digital ID; it's your personal brand, the gateway through which viewers decide whether to follow, engage, or simply scroll past. Understanding the intricacies of profile optimization is paramount in building a loyal and active audience.

Throughout the pages of this chapter, we will delve into the elements that make up a standout TikTok profile. From selecting the perfect profile picture to crafting an attention-grabbing bio, we'll guide you through the process of curating a profile that reflects your personality and resonates with your target audience.

But it doesn't end there. We'll explore the significance of consistency, the power of a memorable username, and the strategic use of links and hashtags to boost your discoverability. As we navigate through the nuances of profile optimization, you'll gain insights into building a brand that not only captures attention but compels viewers to hit that coveted "Follow" button.

So, whether you're a TikTok novice or a seasoned creator looking to refine your online presence, Chapter 3 is your go-to resource for transforming your profile into a magnet for engagement. Let's embark on this journey of self-presentation in the digital realm and unlock the full potential of your TikTok persona. Get ready to optimize, captivate, and leave an indelible mark on the TikTok landscape.

3.1 Creating an Eye-Catching Profile Picture

In the bustling world of TikTok, your profile picture is the first impression, the digital handshake that introduces you to the vast community of viewers. In this section of "Mastering TikTok: A Guide to Creating Viral Videos," we delve into the art of creating an eye-catching profile picture—an essential element in shaping your online identity and attracting the attention your content deserves.

The Importance of First Impressions

In the whirlwind of content consumption on TikTok, first impressions matter. Your profile picture is the first visual cue users encounter when stumbling upon your content, and it serves as a visual anchor that reflects your personality and content style. An eye-catching profile picture not only piques curiosity but also entices viewers to explore your profile and engage with your videos.

Elements of an Effective Profile Picture

1. Clarity and Visibility: Ensure that your profile picture is clear, well-lit, and easily distinguishable, even in a thumbnail size. Avoid clutter and busy backgrounds that may distract from your face or intended focal point.

2. Expressiveness: Let your personality shine through your expression. Whether it's a genuine smile, a confident look, or an expression that aligns with your content style, your profile picture should convey a sense of who you are and what viewers can expect.

3. Consistency with Branding: If you've established a personal brand or a recognizable style in your content, consider aligning your profile picture with that brand. Consistency fosters recognition, making it easier for viewers to remember and identify your profile amidst the sea of content.

4. Composition: Pay attention to the composition of your profile picture. Centering your face, using a close-up shot, and avoiding excessive background distractions are effective strategies for creating a visually appealing and memorable profile image.

Incorporating Creativity

While clarity and expressiveness are crucial, don't shy away from injecting creativity into your profile picture. Consider how you can convey aspects of your content or personality through creative elements. Whether it's incorporating elements related to your niche or utilizing vibrant colors, creativity can make your profile stand out.

Updating and Iterating

Your profile picture is not a static element. As your content evolves and your style develops, consider updating your profile picture to reflect these changes. Regularly reviewing and iterating on your profile picture ensures that it remains a current and accurate representation of your brand on TikTok.

As we conclude our exploration of creating an eye-catching profile picture, remember that your profile is your digital identity on TikTok. Your profile picture, in particular, is a visual ambassador that introduces you to potential followers and collaborators. In the subsequent sections of Chapter 3, we'll continue to optimize your TikTok profile, exploring elements such as bio optimization, link strategy, and the overall aesthetics of your profile. Get ready to make a lasting impression and ensure that your profile becomes a welcoming gateway for viewers to explore the captivating content you've mastered.

3.2 Crafting an Engaging Bio

In the fast-paced world of TikTok, where attention spans are brief and first impressions are vital, your bio is a concise canvas to showcase your personality, interests, and the essence of your content. In this section of "Mastering TikTok: A Guide to Creating Viral Videos," we delve into the art of crafting an engaging bio that not only captivates potential followers but also sets the stage for a meaningful connection.

The Bio's Role in Your TikTok Journey

Your TikTok bio is the narrative snippet that accompanies your profile picture, offering a brief but powerful glimpse into who you are and what viewers can expect from your content. It's a valuable tool for making a compelling case for why users should follow you, setting the tone for your profile, and enticing viewers to explore your videos.

Elements of an Effective TikTok Bio

1. Clarity and Conciseness: Given the limited character count in a TikTok bio, clarity and conciseness are paramount. Clearly communicate your niche, interests, or content theme in a succinct manner. Consider it a digital elevator pitch—make every word count.

2. Personality and Tone: Infuse your bio with your unique personality and the tone that aligns with your content. Whether it's humor, enthusiasm, or a touch of mystery, your bio is an opportunity to convey the vibe of your TikTok persona.

3. Keywords and Hashtags: Incorporate relevant keywords and hashtags related to your niche. This not only aids in discoverability but also helps your profile align with the interests of potential followers. Consider using popular hashtags in your bio that resonate with your content.

4. Calls to Action (CTAs): Encourage engagement by including clear calls to action. Whether it's inviting viewers to like, share, or duet your videos, CTAs prompt interaction and deepen the connection between you and your audience.

5. External Links: If you have the option to include external links, strategically use them to direct viewers to additional content, other social media platforms, or even products and services. Ensure that these links align with your overall brand and content strategy.

Showcasing Achievements and Milestones

If you have noteworthy achievements or milestones, such as hitting a follower milestone, collaborations, or significant moments in your TikTok journey, consider showcasing them in your bio. Not only does this provide social proof of your credibility, but it also signals to potential followers that they are joining a community with a vibrant and evolving story.

Regular Updates and Iterations

Treat your bio as a dynamic element that evolves with your content and personal brand. Regularly revisit and update your bio to reflect changes in your content style, collaborations, or any shifts in your overall brand narrative. An updated bio keeps your profile fresh and relevant.

As we conclude our exploration of crafting an engaging bio on TikTok, remember that your bio is the virtual handshake that introduces you to the TikTok community. In the upcoming sections of Chapter 3, we'll continue to optimize your TikTok profile, exploring strategies for link placement, profile aesthetics, and additional tips to enhance your digital presence. Get ready to make your bio a compelling invitation for viewers to join you on your TikTok journey.

3.3 Linking Other Social Media Profiles

In the interconnected landscape of social media, your TikTok profile serves as a gateway to your broader digital presence. In this section of "Mastering TikTok: A Guide to Creating Viral Videos," we explore the strategic practice of linking other social media profiles to your TikTok account—a move that not only expands your reach but also enhances your online influence.

The Power of Cross-Platform Connectivity

Linking your other social media profiles to your TikTok account creates a digital bridge between platforms, allowing your audience to seamlessly transition from one space to another. This interconnected approach is a powerful strategy for expanding your reach, fostering a cohesive online presence, and leveraging the strengths of each platform to complement your TikTok content.

Choosing Appropriate Platforms

Consider the nature of your content and audience when selecting which social media profiles to link. For example, if your TikTok content is visual or involves lifestyle elements, platforms like Instagram or Pinterest might be suitable. For more professional or business-oriented content, LinkedIn may be a relevant choice. Linking the platforms that align with your brand ensures a consistent experience for your audience.

The TikTok Bio Link

While TikTok typically allows a single link in the bio, you can strategically utilize this link to direct viewers to a landing page where they can find links to all your connected social media profiles. Services like Linktree or personal websites are popular choices for aggregating links. This central hub provides a convenient way for viewers to explore your content across different platforms.

Encouraging Cross-Platform Engagement

Linking other social media profiles not only expands your audience but also encourages cross-platform engagement. Encourage TikTok followers to explore your other platforms for additional content, behind-the-scenes glimpses, or unique offerings. Cross-promotion fosters a sense of community across your digital spaces.

Monitoring Analytics and Performance

Leverage analytics tools available on each platform to monitor the performance of cross-platform linking. Track the traffic and engagement generated from TikTok to your other profiles. This data provides valuable insights into the effectiveness of your strategy and helps refine your approach for optimal results.

Updating Links for Campaigns and Collaborations

If you're running campaigns, promotions, or collaborations across multiple platforms, regularly update your TikTok bio link to reflect these initiatives. This ensures that your TikTok audience has direct access to the latest content, promotions, or collaborative efforts happening on your linked platforms.

As we conclude our exploration of linking other social media profiles to your TikTok account, remember that cross-platform connectivity is a dynamic strategy that evolves with your content and digital presence. In the subsequent sections of Chapter 3, we'll continue to optimize your TikTok profile, exploring additional strategies for profile aesthetics, engagement, and overall brand cohesion. Get ready to unlock the full potential of your interconnected digital journey.

Chapter 4: Leveraging TikTok Features

Welcome to Chapter 4 of "Mastering TikTok: A Guide to Creating Viral Videos." As we continue our exploration of the dynamic world of TikTok, we now shift our focus to the myriad features that this platform offers. In this chapter, aptly titled "Leveraging TikTok Features," we'll uncover the tools and functionalities that can elevate your content, increase engagement, and amplify your presence within the TikTok community.

TikTok is more than just a video-sharing platform; it's a treasure trove of creative possibilities waiting to be unlocked. From duets and challenges to filters and effects, each feature has the potential to add a unique dimension to your videos and enhance your storytelling capabilities. In this chapter, we'll guide you through the diverse array of features, helping you harness their power to create content that not only captivates but resonates with your audience.

Get ready to explore the art of collaboration through duets, where your creativity can merge seamlessly with that of fellow TikTok creators. Uncover the secrets behind trending challenges and learn how to seamlessly integrate them into your content strategy. We'll also delve into the world of effects and filters, showcasing how these tools can add flair, personality, and visual appeal to your videos.

But it doesn't stop there. From TikTok's innovative editing tools to the nuances of live streaming, we'll equip you with the knowledge to navigate and leverage each feature strategically. Whether you're aiming to entertain, educate, or inspire, this chapter will empower you to use TikTok's features to your advantage, creating a dynamic and engaging content experience for your audience.

So, whether you're a TikTok enthusiast looking to expand your creative repertoire or a budding creator seeking to maximize the potential of this platform, Chapter 4 is your guide to mastering the features that set TikTok apart. Let's dive into the exciting realm of TikTok features and discover how they can propel your content to new heights of virality and impact.

4.1 Exploring Filters and Effects

In the vibrant tapestry of TikTok creativity, filters and effects are the palette that allows creators to paint their videos with a spectrum of visual enchantment. Welcome to Chapter 4 of "Mastering TikTok: A Guide to Creating Viral Videos," where we delve into the art of exploring filters and effects—a transformative element that can elevate your content, captivate viewers, and set your videos apart in the dynamic landscape of TikTok.

The Visual Language of TikTok

TikTok's vast array of filters and effects is a testament to the platform's commitment to visual storytelling. These tools allow creators to infuse their content with creativity, add layers to their narratives, and create a visual identity that resonates with their audience. Understanding and harnessing the power of filters and effects is a strategic move in the pursuit of TikTok mastery.

Navigating the Filter Library

TikTok's filter library is a treasure trove of visual enhancements, ranging from subtle color corrections to whimsical face-altering effects. Spend time exploring the available filters to discover those that align with your content style and niche. Whether it's a vintage aesthetic, a dreamlike glow, or a dynamic glitch effect, filters can contribute to the visual consistency of your videos.

Leveraging Special Effects

Special effects, such as transitions, animations, and augmented reality elements, add a touch of magic to your TikTok content. Experiment with the diverse range of special effects to bring your ideas to life. Whether it's a seamless transition between scenes, a burst of confetti, or a fantastical background, these effects can captivate viewers and make your videos memorable.

Enhancing Storytelling with Effects

Filters and effects aren't just cosmetic enhancements; they are storytelling tools. Consider how specific effects can enhance the narrative arc of your content. For example, using a slow-motion effect for dramatic moments or a fast-paced transition for comedic punchlines can add a dynamic layer to your storytelling, creating a more engaging and immersive viewer experience.

Trending Effects and Challenges

TikTok is a platform driven by trends, and effects often play a central role in these trends. Stay attuned to trending effects and challenges, and consider how you can incorporate them into your content. Whether it's a dance trend with a specific filter or a challenge that encourages creative use of effects, participating in these trends can boost your visibility and engagement.

Personalizing Your Visual Style

While exploring the myriad of filters and effects, consider how you can personalize them to align with your visual style. Adjusting the intensity, combining multiple effects, or even creating your own signature look can contribute to the uniqueness of your videos. A distinctive visual style becomes a recognizable element of your brand on TikTok.

As we conclude our exploration of exploring filters and effects on TikTok, remember that these tools are not just embellishments but integral components of your creative toolkit. In the upcoming sections of Chapter 4, we'll continue to unravel the features of TikTok, exploring strategies for music integration, text overlays, and additional elements that contribute to the mastery of the TikTok platform. Get ready to infuse your videos with visual magic and unlock the full spectrum of creative possibilities on TikTok.

4.2 Using Duet and Stitch Features

In the symphony of TikTok collaboration, the Duet and Stitch features are the instruments that allow creators to harmonize, remix, and co-create content. Welcome to Chapter 4 of "Mastering TikTok: A Guide to Creating Viral Videos," where we explore the dynamic art of using Duet and Stitch features—a collaborative dance that opens the door to new creative dimensions and fosters connections within the TikTok community.

Duet: A Creative Pas de Deux

The Duet feature on TikTok is a creative partnership that enables you to collaborate with other creators. Whether it's dancing side by side, reacting to content, or participating in a duet challenge, this feature allows you to share the screen with fellow creators and create content that seamlessly blends two perspectives. Duetting is not just a shared performance; it's an opportunity to tap into the collaborative spirit of TikTok.

Navigating Duet Challenges

Duet challenges are a popular trend on TikTok, where creators participate in a collective theme or dance, showcasing their individual interpretations side by side. Engaging with Duet challenges not only connects you with a broader community but also exposes your content to a wider audience as users explore and engage with the collaborative responses to the challenge.

Leveraging Split Screen Creativity

Duet offers a split-screen format that allows for visual storytelling, interaction, and even comedic exchanges between creators. Experiment with creative uses of the split screen—whether it's a virtual dialogue, a storytelling collaboration, or a visually synchronized performance. The split-screen format opens doors to endless possibilities for collaborative content.

Stitch: Weaving Narratives Together

The Stitch feature on TikTok takes collaboration a step further by allowing you to "stitch" your video to someone else's, creating a seamless transition between the two. This feature is a powerful tool for building on existing content, adding your perspective, or responding directly to another creator's video. Stitching fosters a sense of interconnected storytelling within the TikTok community.

Tapping into Trending Stitches

Similar to Duet challenges, Stitch challenges are prevalent on TikTok, where creators are encouraged to contribute their unique stitches to a trending theme or narrative. Participating in these challenges not only provides an opportunity for collaboration but also positions your content within the currents of TikTok trends, enhancing discoverability and engagement.

Creative Collaboration Strategies

When using Duet and Stitch features, consider strategic approaches to maximize creative collaboration:

1. Aligning with Niche Creators: Collaborate with creators in your niche or those who share similar interests. This alignment ensures that the collaboration feels authentic and resonates with both audiences.

2. Interactive Storytelling: Use Duet and Stitch to create interactive storytelling experiences. Invite viewers to participate in choosing the direction of the narrative, reacting to content, or contributing their perspectives.

3. Showcasing Talents: Collaborate with creators who bring unique talents to the table. Whether it's showcasing dance skills, artistic abilities, or expert knowledge, diverse collaborations add depth to your content.

As we conclude our exploration of using Duet and Stitch features on TikTok, remember that collaboration is not just a feature; it's a dynamic aspect of TikTok culture. In the upcoming sections of Chapter 4, we'll continue to uncover the features of TikTok, exploring strategies for integrating music, incorporating text overlays, and additional elements that contribute to TikTok mastery. Get ready to dance, stitch, and co-create your way to a vibrant TikTok presence.

4.3 Understanding Challenges and Hashtags

In the dynamic world of TikTok, challenges and hashtags are the rallying points where creators converge, showcase their creativity, and ride the waves of viral trends. Welcome to Chapter 4 of "Mastering TikTok: A Guide to Creating Viral Videos," where we unravel the intricate dance of understanding challenges and hashtags—a strategic endeavor that propels your content into the limelight and connects you with the vibrant TikTok community.

The Pulse of TikTok: Challenges

Challenges are the heartbeat of TikTok, driving trends, inspiring creativity, and uniting creators in a shared experience. Participating in challenges not only aligns your content with the currents of TikTok culture but also positions it for increased visibility through the platform's algorithm. Challenges are thematic prompts that invite creators to contribute their unique interpretations, whether through dance, lip-syncing, or creative expressions.

Navigating Popular Challenges

Staying attuned to popular challenges is a strategic move for TikTok success. The Discover Page, where trending content is showcased, is a gateway to discovering and engaging with the latest challenges. Exploring and participating in these challenges not only connects you with the broader TikTok community but also exposes your content to a wider audience, increasing the likelihood of appearing on the coveted For You Page.

Crafting Original Challenges

While participating in existing challenges is valuable, crafting your original challenges can set you apart as a trendsetter. Original challenges allow you to infuse your creativity into TikTok culture, potentially sparking a trend that others join. When creating challenges, consider themes that align with your niche, showcase your unique style, and invite diverse interpretations. A successful original challenge not only engages your existing audience but also attracts new participants.

The Power of Hashtags

Hashtags are the language of TikTok, providing a means of categorization, discovery, and community building. Incorporating relevant hashtags into your captions and bio is essential for ensuring that your content aligns with the interests of your target audience. Strategic use of hashtags also enhances the discoverability of your content, allowing it to surface on users' For You Pages who engage with similar themes.

Participating in Hashtag Trends

Beyond creating your own challenges, participating in hashtag trends is an effective strategy for expanding your reach. Keep an eye on trending hashtags and explore how you can incorporate them into your content. Trending hashtags not only connect your content with wider conversations but also position it to capitalize on the visibility generated by popular trends.

Creating Branded Hashtags

For creators with established personal brands, creating branded hashtags is a powerful strategy for community building and content aggregation. Branded hashtags encourage your audience to contribute content under a shared theme, fostering a sense of belonging and creating a curated collection of user-generated content that aligns with your brand.

As we conclude our exploration of understanding challenges and hashtags on TikTok, remember that these elements are the threads that weave the fabric of TikTok culture. In the upcoming sections of Chapter 4, we'll continue to uncover the features of TikTok, exploring strategies for integrating music, incorporating text overlays, and additional elements that contribute to TikTok mastery. Get ready to dance to the rhythm of challenges, ride the waves of hashtags, and immerse yourself in the vibrant tapestry of TikTok trends.

Chapter 5: Consistency and Timing

Welcome to Chapter 5 of "Mastering TikTok: A Guide to Creating Viral Videos." In the fast-paced and ever-evolving world of TikTok, two key elements play a pivotal role in the success of any creator: consistency and timing. As we delve into this chapter, appropriately titled "Consistency and Timing," we'll unravel the significance of maintaining a regular content cadence and strategically timing your uploads to optimize visibility and engagement.

Consistency is the backbone of a thriving TikTok presence. It goes beyond the frequency of your uploads; it's about establishing a rhythm that your audience can rely on. In this chapter, we'll explore the importance of a consistent posting schedule, helping you strike the right balance between quality and quantity. Whether you're a full-time creator or navigating TikTok alongside other commitments, we'll provide insights into crafting a sustainable content strategy that keeps your audience eagerly anticipating your next creation.

Timing is everything in the world of TikTok, where trends can surge and fade in the blink of an eye. Understanding when to post your videos can significantly impact their reach and engagement. We'll dive into the nuances of TikTok's algorithm, shedding light on the optimal times to share your content for maximum visibility. Additionally, we'll explore the relevance of staying attuned to cultural events, holidays, and trending topics to amplify the impact of your videos.

But it's not just about being consistent in your posting schedule and timing; it's also about maintaining a cohesive narrative and visual identity. We'll guide you through the art of thematic consistency, helping you create a brand that resonates with your audience and sets you apart in the crowded TikTok landscape.

Whether you're a seasoned TikTok creator seeking to refine your approach or a newcomer looking to establish a strong foundation, Chapter 5 is your compass for navigating the temporal dimensions of TikTok success. Let's explore the symbiotic relationship between consistency and timing, and harness their power to propel your TikTok journey to new heights of influence and virality.

5.1 Establishing a Posting Schedule

In the ever-evolving dance of TikTok, consistency is the rhythm that keeps your audience engaged, and timing is the choreography that ensures your content takes center stage. Welcome to Chapter 5 of "Mastering TikTok: A Guide to Creating Viral Videos," where we explore the art of establishing a posting schedule—a strategic endeavor that not only nurtures your relationship with followers but also maximizes the impact of your content on the TikTok algorithm.

The Importance of Consistency

Consistency is the backbone of a successful TikTok presence. When followers know what to expect and when to expect it, they are more likely to engage with your content regularly. Establishing a posting schedule creates a sense of anticipation, fostering a connection with your audience and making your profile a regular destination for their TikTok journey.

Frequency and Timing

Determining how often to post and the optimal times for your content is a delicate balance that depends on your audience, niche, and content style. While there is no one-size-fits-all approach, consider the following factors when establishing your posting schedule:

1. Audience Behavior: Analyze when your target audience is most active on TikTok. Experiment with posting at different times and days to identify patterns of peak engagement.

2. Niche Trends: Consider the trends within your niche. If your content aligns with specific trends or challenges, timing your posts to coincide with the popularity of these trends can enhance visibility.

3. Global Audience: If your audience spans different time zones, aim for a posting schedule that accommodates various regions. This ensures that your content is accessible to a broader audience.

4. Consistent Frequency: Whether you choose to post daily, a few times a week, or on specific days, maintain a consistent frequency. Regularity builds anticipation and helps your audience incorporate your content into their TikTok routine.

Utilizing TikTok Analytics

TikTok provides analytics tools that offer insights into the performance of your content. Utilize these analytics to assess the effectiveness of your posting schedule. Monitor when your audience is most active, identify peak engagement times, and adjust your posting schedule based on data-driven insights.

Experimentation and Adaptation

The TikTok landscape is dynamic, and audience behavior can change over time. Don't be afraid to experiment with different posting schedules to gauge audience response. Pay attention to the performance metrics of your videos and adapt your schedule based on evolving trends and audience engagement patterns.

Building Anticipation with Teasers

Enhance the anticipation surrounding your content by teasing upcoming posts. Use your TikTok Stories or captions to hint at what's coming next. Building excitement around your content encourages followers to stay tuned and actively seek out your videos when they drop.

As we conclude our exploration of establishing a posting schedule on TikTok, remember that consistency is the heartbeat of a thriving TikTok presence. In the subsequent sections of Chapter 5, we'll continue to unravel the intricacies of consistency and timing, exploring strategies for maintaining content quality, optimizing video length, and additional elements that contribute to TikTok mastery. Get ready to set the stage for a rhythmic and impactful TikTok journey.

5.2 Analyzing Peak Engagement Times

In the dynamic realm of TikTok, understanding when your audience is most active is akin to finding the perfect tempo for your dance. Welcome to Chapter 5 of "Mastering TikTok: A Guide to Creating Viral Videos," where we delve into the strategic art of analyzing peak engagement times—a nuanced exploration that ensures your content resonates with your audience when the spotlight is brightest.

The TikTok Rhythm: Peak Engagement

Peak engagement times refer to the periods when your audience is most active and receptive to content. Identifying and capitalizing on these windows of opportunity is crucial for maximizing the impact of your videos and increasing the likelihood of landing on the coveted For You Page.

Utilizing TikTok Analytics

TikTok offers a robust analytics platform that provides valuable insights into your audience's behavior. Navigate to your TikTok Pro account to access analytics tools, including data on when your followers are most active. Key metrics include:

1. Follower Activity: Analyze the Follower Activity section to understand the days and times when your followers are most active on TikTok. This data provides a foundation for crafting a posting schedule aligned with audience behavior.

2. Video Views and Engagement: Explore the performance metrics of your past videos, paying attention to views, likes, shares, and comments. Identify patterns in engagement based on the time of day and day of the week.

Experimenting with Posting Times

While analytics provide valuable guidance, it's essential to experiment with posting times to fine-tune your schedule. Consider the following strategies:

1. Testing Different Time Slots: Experiment with posting at various times throughout the day and different days of the week. Assess the performance of your videos during these testing phases to identify optimal time slots.

2. Time Zone Considerations: If your audience spans different time zones, factor in the global distribution of your followers. Aim for a posting schedule that accommodates peak engagement times across diverse regions.

3. Consistency in Experimentation: When testing different posting times, maintain consistency in other variables, such as content style and video length. This ensures that the impact on engagement is primarily attributed to the timing variable.

Tailoring to Your Niche

Consider the nature of your content and its alignment with niche trends. For example, if your content is related to morning routines or evening activities, adjust your posting times to coincide with these themes. Tailoring your schedule to your niche increases the relevance of your content to your audience.

The Role of Time Zones

The global reach of TikTok means that your audience might be scattered across different time zones. Leverage the insights from TikTok analytics to create a posting schedule that accommodates peak engagement times in various regions. This approach ensures that your content is accessible to a broader international audience.

As we conclude our exploration of analyzing peak engagement times on TikTok, remember that timing is a dynamic element influenced by audience behavior, content style, and global distribution. In the subsequent sections of Chapter 5, we'll continue to unravel the intricacies of consistency and timing, exploring strategies for maintaining content quality, optimizing video length, and additional elements that contribute to TikTok mastery. Get ready to fine-tune the rhythm of your TikTok journey and synchronize with the heartbeat of your audience.

Chapter 6: Engaging with the TikTok Community

Welcome to Chapter 6 of "Mastering TikTok: A Guide to Creating Viral Videos." In the vibrant and interconnected world of TikTok, success isn't just about creating exceptional content; it's about fostering meaningful connections within the community. As we embark on this chapter, aptly titled "Engaging with the TikTok Community," we'll unravel the art of building relationships, participating in trends, and cultivating a loyal following that extends beyond your videos.

TikTok is not just a platform; it's a thriving community of creators, viewers, and trends that shape the cultural landscape. In this chapter, we'll explore the various facets of community engagement, from understanding the power of comments and duets to participating in challenges that transcend individual boundaries. Through practical insights and real-world examples, we'll guide you in navigating the nuances of community dynamics and help you forge connections that can amplify your reach and impact.

Discover the art of responding to comments, fostering a positive and interactive dialogue with your audience. Uncover the potential of duets as a collaborative tool to connect with fellow creators, and learn how to leverage challenges not only for personal growth but also to contribute to the larger TikTok conversation.

We'll delve into the importance of authenticity in community engagement, showcasing how being genuine and approachable can turn viewers into dedicated followers. From shoutouts to collaborations, we'll provide strategies to elevate your engagement game and become an active participant in the TikTok ecosystem.

Whether you're a TikTok veteran or a newcomer eager to establish your presence, Chapter 6 serves as your guide to unlocking the full potential of community engagement. Let's explore the symbiotic relationship between creators and viewers, understand the pulse of TikTok trends, and foster connections that transform your journey from solo content creation to a shared experience within the dynamic TikTok community. Get ready to engage, connect, and make your mark beyond the confines of your videos.

6.1 Responding to Comments and Messages

In the lively and interactive landscape of TikTok, engagement is the heartbeat that sustains your connection with the community. Welcome to Chapter 6 of "Mastering TikTok: A Guide to Creating Viral Videos," where we dive into the art of responding to comments and messages—a crucial aspect that not only strengthens your bond with followers but also cultivates a vibrant and participatory TikTok presence.

The Significance of Engagement

Engagement is a two-way street on TikTok, with creators and followers actively participating in a dialogue. Responding to comments and messages is more than a courtesy; it's an opportunity to humanize your profile, build relationships, and create a sense of community. The TikTok algorithm also favors content that generates meaningful interactions, making engagement a strategic move for increased visibility.

Acknowledging and Appreciating

Responding to comments is a simple yet powerful way to acknowledge the time and effort your audience invests in engaging with your content. Whether it's a compliment, a question, or a creative remark, taking the time to respond demonstrates appreciation and fosters a positive atmosphere within your TikTok community.

Prompt Responses

In the fast-paced world of TikTok, prompt responses enhance the interactive experience. Aim to respond to comments and messages in a timely manner, especially during the initial hours after posting a video. This not only capitalizes on the momentum generated by your content but also makes your profile feel dynamic and engaged.

Encouraging Dialogue

Initiate and encourage dialogue within the comments section. Pose questions, seek opinions, or invite viewers to share their thoughts. Active engagement invites more participation, creating a dynamic conversation around your content. Responding to comments not only fosters a sense of community but also signals to the TikTok algorithm that your content is generating discussion.

Handling Negative Comments

In the diverse TikTok community, encountering a range of opinions is inevitable. When faced with negative comments, approach them with professionalism and empathy. Address constructive criticism with gratitude, and consider ignoring or gently redirecting unwarranted negativity. Responding calmly and respectfully demonstrates maturity and can turn a negative interaction into a positive one.

Leveraging TikTok Messages

Direct messages (DMs) are a private channel for one-on-one communication with your audience. Responding to DMs provides a personalized touch and offers an opportunity to connect with followers on a deeper level. Consider the following when engaging through messages:

1. Personalization: Tailor your responses to individual messages, acknowledging specific comments or inquiries. Personalization fosters a stronger sense of connection.

2. Encouraging User-Generated Content: Use messages to encourage followers to create and share content related to your niche or challenges. This not only boosts engagement but also showcases user-generated content on your profile.

3. Responding to Collaborations: If you receive collaboration requests or partnership inquiries, respond promptly and professionally. Collaborations can expand your reach and introduce your content to new audiences.

Maintaining a Positive Tone

TikTok is a platform where positivity and creativity thrive. Maintain a positive and enthusiastic tone in your responses. Your interactions contribute to the overall atmosphere of your profile, influencing how viewers perceive your content and community.

As we conclude our exploration of responding to comments and messages on TikTok, remember that engagement is the heartbeat of a thriving TikTok presence. In the upcoming sections of Chapter 6, we'll continue to unravel the intricacies of engaging with the TikTok community, exploring strategies for collaborations, handling trends, and additional elements that contribute to TikTok mastery. Get ready to immerse yourself in the vibrant dialogue of TikTok and cultivate meaningful connections with your audience.

6.2 Collaborating with Other TikTok Creators

In the symphony of creativity that is TikTok, collaboration is the key to creating harmonies that resonate across the platform. Welcome to Chapter 6 of "Mastering TikTok: A Guide to Creating Viral Videos," where we explore the dynamic art of collaborating with other TikTok creators—an endeavor that not only expands your reach but also infuses your content with fresh perspectives, fostering a sense of community and shared creativity.

The Power of TikTok Collaboration

Collaboration on TikTok is more than just a shared performance; it's a dynamic exchange of ideas, styles, and audiences. Whether it's a duet, a stitching response, or a joint challenge, collaborating with other creators introduces diversity into your content, exposes your profile to new audiences, and strengthens the sense of community within the TikTok ecosystem.

Identifying Collaborative Opportunities

Discovering collaborative opportunities requires a keen eye for trends, niches, and content styles that align with your own. Consider the following strategies:

1. Explore Your Niche: Identify creators within your niche or those with complementary content styles. Collaborating with creators who share similar interests ensures that the partnership feels authentic and resonates with both audiences.

2. Participate in Challenges: TikTok challenges often present ideal collaboration opportunities. Engage with challenges and explore collaborations within the challenge framework. This not only aligns your content with trends but also provides a shared theme for collaboration.

3. Leverage Discovery Page: The Discovery Page is a hub of trending and popular content. Explore this page to discover creators whose content aligns with yours. Reach out to potential collaborators by commenting on their videos or sending direct messages expressing interest in collaboration.

The Art of Duets

Duets are a distinctive form of collaboration on TikTok, allowing you to share the screen with another creator. Here's how to make the most of duet collaborations:

1. Reacting and Responding: Use duets to react to another creator's video, respond to challenges, or showcase a side-by-side performance. Duets are an excellent medium for creative expression and shared storytelling.

2. Incorporating Split-Screen Creativity: Experiment with the split-screen format in duets. Whether it's a virtual conversation, a collaborative performance, or a synchronized dance, the split-screen provides opportunities for visually engaging content.

3. Aligning Aesthetics: Coordinate with your collaborator to align aesthetics, themes, or even color schemes. A visually cohesive collaboration enhances the overall impact and creates a seamless viewing experience for your audience.

Stitching and Responding

Stitching is another collaboration feature on TikTok that enables you to "stitch" your video to another creator's, creating a continuous narrative. Consider the following when stitching and responding:

1. Building on Ideas: Use stitching to build on ideas presented in another creator's video. This allows you to contribute your perspective, showcase additional content, or offer a unique take on a theme.

2. Showcasing Expertise: If another creator has shared content related to your expertise or niche, use stitching as a way to showcase your knowledge, add value, or provide additional insights. This not only benefits your collaborator but also positions you as an authority in your niche.

Communication and Coordination

Effective collaboration requires clear communication and coordination with your collaborator. Consider the following tips:

1. Establishing Goals: Clearly define the goals and objectives of the collaboration. Whether it's to entertain, educate, or contribute to a specific challenge, a shared understanding ensures a cohesive collaboration.

2. Setting Guidelines: Establish guidelines for content style, tone, and any specific elements you want to incorporate. Guidelines provide a framework for creativity and ensure that the collaboration aligns with both creators' visions.

3. Mutual Promotion: Collaborate on promotion strategies. Cross-promote each other's content by tagging, mentioning, or creating teaser videos leading up to the collaboration. This mutual promotion extends the reach of the collaboration to both creators' audiences.

As we conclude our exploration of collaborating with other TikTok creators, remember that collaboration is a dynamic and enriching aspect of TikTok culture. In the subsequent sections of Chapter 6, we'll continue to unravel the intricacies of engaging with the TikTok community, exploring strategies for handling trends, participating in challenges, and additional elements that contribute to TikTok mastery. Get ready to dance, stitch, and collaborate your way to a vibrant and interconnected TikTok presence.

6.3 Participating in Challenges

In the dynamic landscape of TikTok, challenges are the beating heart that unites creators, sparks creativity, and propels trends to the forefront of the platform. Welcome to Chapter 6 of "Mastering TikTok: A Guide to Creating Viral Videos," where we explore the exhilarating world of participating in challenges—an endeavor that not only connects you with the TikTok community but also positions your content at the epicenter of viral trends.

Embracing TikTok Culture: The Challenge Phenomenon

Challenges on TikTok are more than just prompts; they are cultural phenomena that sweep through the platform, inviting creators to showcase their interpretations, talents, and creativity. Participating in challenges not only immerses you in TikTok culture but also offers a strategic avenue for expanding your reach, increasing discoverability, and establishing your presence within the community.

Navigating the Discover Page

The Discover Page is a gateway to TikTok's trending content, featuring a curated selection of challenges and popular videos. Explore this page regularly to discover the latest challenges, trends, and themes that resonate with your interests and niche. Engaging with challenges from the Discover Page provides visibility and connects your content with the broader TikTok community.

The Art of Participation

When participating in challenges, consider the following strategies to maximize your impact:

1. Adding Your Unique Twist: Challenges often attract a multitude of participants. Differentiate your contribution by adding a unique twist, whether it's a creative variation, a personal touch, or a novel approach to the challenge theme.

2. Showcasing Your Strengths: Choose challenges that align with your strengths and showcase your talents. Whether it's dancing, lip-syncing, comedy, or a niche-specific challenge, leveraging your strengths enhances the quality and authenticity of your participation.

3. Engaging with the Challenge Theme: Immerse yourself in the challenge theme and incorporate it seamlessly into your content. Whether the challenge is based on a dance, a trend, or a specific topic, aligning with the theme ensures that your contribution resonates with the challenge's intended narrative.

Trending Challenges and Hashtags

TikTok's dynamic nature means that challenges and hashtags trend rapidly. Stay attuned to the latest trends by monitoring the For You Page, following popular creators, and exploring the Discover Page. Participating in trending challenges increases the visibility of your content, exposes it to a wider audience, and positions your videos within the currents of TikTok culture.

Leveraging Duets and Stitches in Challenges

Enhance your challenge participation by incorporating duets and stitches. Reacting to other creators' challenge entries through duets or stitches adds an interactive layer to your content and fosters collaboration within the TikTok community. This collaborative approach not only amplifies the challenge's impact but also connects you with other creators.

Creating Your Own Challenges

As a creator, you have the power to initiate and lead challenges. Crafting your challenges allows you to infuse TikTok culture with your unique perspective, engage with your audience, and potentially spark trends. When creating challenges, consider the following:

1. Clear Instructions: Provide clear and concise instructions for your challenge. Clarity ensures that participants understand the theme, allowing for diverse and creative interpretations.

2. Engagement Strategies: Encourage participants to engage with your challenge by liking, commenting, and duetting with entries. Actively participating in the challenge you've created fosters a sense of community and strengthens your connection with followers.

3. Promotion and Recognition: Promote your challenge through teaser videos, mentions, and collaborations with other creators. Recognize and acknowledge participants by duetting with their entries, showcasing them in your videos, or even dedicating a video to highlight standout contributions.

As we conclude our exploration of participating in challenges on TikTok, remember that challenges are the lifeblood of TikTok culture. In the upcoming sections of Chapter 6, we'll continue to unravel the intricacies of engaging with the TikTok community, exploring strategies for handling trends, optimizing collaborations, and additional elements that contribute to TikTok mastery. Get ready to immerse yourself in the ever-evolving tapestry of TikTok challenges and let your creativity shine in the vibrant chorus of the TikTok community.

Chapter 7: Analyzing Analytics

Welcome to Chapter 7 of "Mastering TikTok: A Guide to Creating Viral Videos." In the realm of TikTok mastery, knowledge is power, and understanding the metrics behind your content is paramount. In this chapter, appropriately titled "Analyzing Analytics," we'll dive into the world of data-driven insights, equipping you with the tools to decipher TikTok analytics and leverage them to refine your content strategy.

TikTok, like any dynamic social platform, provides a wealth of data that can illuminate the performance of your videos. From views and likes to audience demographics and watch time, these analytics offer a roadmap to understanding what resonates with your audience and how to optimize for even greater success.

In this chapter, we'll guide you through the intricacies of TikTok analytics, breaking down key metrics and shedding light on their implications for your content. Learn how to interpret the data behind your video views, discover the significance of engagement metrics, and unearth the secrets to identifying your core audience.

But it's not just about decoding the numbers; it's about using that knowledge to refine your content creation strategy. We'll explore how analytics can inform your decision-making process, from tailoring your posting schedule to fine-tuning the themes and styles that resonate most with your viewers.

Whether you're a data enthusiast or someone new to the world of analytics, Chapter 7 is your gateway to unlocking the potential of TikTok insights. As we navigate through the metrics and graphs, you'll gain a comprehensive understanding of your TikTok performance and discover how to turn data into actionable strategies for sustained growth and viral success. Get ready to dive into the analytics, refine your approach, and take your TikTok mastery to the next level.

7.1 Understanding TikTok Analytics

In the dynamic universe of TikTok, knowledge is power, and analytics serve as the compass guiding creators on their journey to mastery. Welcome to Chapter 7 of "Mastering TikTok: A Guide to Creating Viral Videos," where we delve into the realm of TikTok Analytics—an essential tool that unveils insights into your audience, content performance, and the intricate dance of the algorithm.

Unlocking the TikTok Pro Account

Before delving into analytics, ensure that you've upgraded to a TikTok Pro account. This unlocks a suite of tools that provides valuable data to inform your content strategy. To switch to a Pro account, navigate to your account settings, select "Manage Account," and then choose "Switch to Pro Account."

Key Metrics in TikTok Analytics

1. Overview: The Overview section provides a snapshot of your account performance, including your profile views, video views, and follower count. This high-level overview gives you an immediate sense of your TikTok presence's health and growth.

2. Followers: The Followers tab offers insights into your audience demographics, including age, gender, location, and the active hours of your followers. Understanding your audience composition is crucial for tailoring content to their preferences and optimizing posting schedules.

3. Content: The Content tab is a treasure trove of data related to your video performance. It includes metrics such as total views, average watch time, and traffic sources. Dive into this section to identify your top-performing videos and analyze viewer engagement.

4. Trends: Stay ahead of the curve by exploring the Trends tab. This section highlights trending hashtags and challenges, allowing you to align your content with the latest TikTok culture and boost discoverability.

5. Discovery: The Discovery tab unveils how viewers discover your content. Analyze metrics such as impressions, reach, and interactions to understand how your videos surface on the For You Page and explore ways to optimize visibility.

Understanding Engagement Metrics

1. Likes: The number of likes your videos receive indicates the level of positive engagement. Pay attention to which videos garner the most likes to identify content themes that resonate with your audience.

2. Comments: Comments are a goldmine of audience feedback. Analyze the type of comments your videos receive—whether they express enjoyment, ask questions, or provide suggestions. Responding to comments fosters community engagement.

3. Shares: Shares signify that viewers find your content compelling enough to share with their own followers. Track the videos with the highest share counts to understand the elements that encourage users to share your content.

4. Watch Time: Watch time measures the total duration viewers spend watching your videos. Longer watch times signal engaging content. Identify videos with high watch times and analyze the storytelling techniques or features that captivate your audience.

Leveraging Analytics for Strategy

1. Identifying Trends: Use analytics to identify trends within your top-performing videos. Analyze common themes, content styles, or hashtags to identify trends that resonate with your audience and incorporate them into future content.

2. Optimizing Content Strategy: Tailor your content strategy based on analytics insights. Adjust the frequency of posting, experiment with different content styles, and refine your approach based on the performance metrics of your videos.

3. Fine-Tuning Posting Schedule: Analyze the active hours of your audience to fine-tune your posting schedule. Aim to post during peak engagement times to maximize visibility and capitalize on optimal audience activity.

4. Collaboration Opportunities: Explore the Followers tab to understand your audience's interests. Identify potential collaborators whose content aligns with your niche and audience demographics. Collaboration based on analytics insights can enhance engagement and expand your reach.

Monitoring Trends and Challenges

1. Discovering Trending Content: The Trends tab provides real-time information on trending content and challenges. Stay updated on the latest trends to align your content with popular themes and enhance discoverability.

2. Crafting Trend-Responsive Content: Analyze the performance of your trend-responsive content. Identify which trends generate the most engagement and replicate successful approaches in future videos to stay in tune with TikTok culture.

As we conclude our exploration of understanding TikTok Analytics, remember that analytics are the compass guiding your TikTok journey. In the upcoming sections of Chapter 7, we'll continue to unravel the intricacies of analyzing analytics, exploring strategies for content optimization, leveraging data-driven insights, and additional elements that contribute to TikTok mastery. Get ready to navigate the vast expanse of TikTok with precision, armed with the insights gleaned from TikTok Analytics.

7.2 Adjusting Strategies Based on Data

In the intricate dance of TikTok, analytics serve as the choreographer's notes, guiding creators to refine their steps and enhance their performance. Welcome to Chapter 7 of "Mastering TikTok: A Guide to Creating Viral Videos," where we explore the art of adjusting strategies based on TikTok Analytics—a dynamic process that transforms raw data into actionable insights, propelling your content toward the forefront of the TikTok stage.

The Strategic Dance with Data

Analytics on TikTok are not mere numbers; they are the pulse of your content's journey. Adjusting strategies based on data involves interpreting the analytics dance to refine your approach, amplify strengths, and address areas for improvement. Here's how to choreograph your TikTok strategy with precision:

1. Identify Top-Performing Content

Dive into the Content tab of TikTok Analytics to identify your top-performing videos. Look beyond raw view counts; consider metrics like average watch time, likes, comments, and shares. Identify patterns in the content style, themes, or storytelling techniques that resonate with your audience.

Action Steps:
- Content Themes: Identify common themes or topics in your top-performing videos.
- Engagement Patterns: Analyze viewer engagement metrics for insights into captivating content

elements.
- Refinement Opportunities: Consider how you can replicate successful content elements in future videos.

2. Understand Audience Demographics

Navigate to the Followers tab to gain insights into your audience's demographics. Analyze age, gender, and location data to understand who comprises your TikTok community. Tailor your content to align with the interests and preferences of your audience, ensuring it resonates with their demographic characteristics.

Action Steps:
- Demographic Insights: Identify key demographic details, including age groups and geographical locations.
- Content Personalization: Tailor your content to match the interests and preferences of your primary audience.
- Explore New Niches: Consider exploring niche content that aligns with your audience's demographics.

3. Refine Posting Schedule

Examine the active hours of your followers to optimize your posting schedule. Post content during peak engagement times to increase visibility and capitalize on the moments when your audience is most active on TikTok.

Action Steps:
- Peak Engagement Times: Identify the days and hours when your audience is most active on TikTok.
- Consistent Posting: Refine your posting schedule to align with peak engagement times for optimal visibility.
- Experiment and Adapt: Test different posting times and days to adapt to evolving audience behavior.

4. Evaluate Hashtag and Challenge Performance

In the Discovery tab, explore how viewers discover your content. Assess the performance of your content using hashtags and challenges. Identify trends in the hashtags that resonate with your audience and contribute to increased discoverability.

Action Steps:
- Hashtag Effectiveness: Evaluate the performance of videos associated with specific hashtags.
- Challenge Participation: Analyze the impact of participating in challenges on your content's visibility.
- Strategic Tagging: Incorporate effective hashtags and challenges into your content strategy for increased discoverability.

5. Experiment with Content Styles

Analytics provide a window into the preferences of your audience. Use this information to experiment with different content styles, whether it's educational, entertaining, or a unique blend that reflects your personality. Gauge audience response to refine your content strategy continually.

Action Steps:
- Content Experimentation: Test different content styles and formats to gauge audience response.
- Iterative Improvement: Use analytics data to iterate and refine your content strategy over time.
- A/B Testing: Experiment with variations of content to identify the most effective approaches.

6. Collaborate Strategically

Leverage analytics insights to identify potential collaborators whose content aligns with your audience. Analyze the Followers tab to discover creators with similar demographics and interests. Collaborate strategically to cross-pollinate audiences and amplify engagement.

Action Steps:
- Collaborator Identification: Identify creators with similar audience demographics and content themes.
- Audience Cross-Pollination: Collaborate with creators to reach new audiences and enhance engagement.
- Strategic Partnerships: Choose collaborators based on shared goals and mutual benefit.

7. Stay Nimble and Adaptive

TikTok's landscape is dynamic, and audience behavior evolves. Stay nimble and adaptive in adjusting your strategies based on emerging trends, cultural shifts, and changes in TikTok algorithms. Continuously monitor analytics to ensure your strategies remain aligned with audience preferences.

Action Steps:
- Trend Monitoring: Stay informed about emerging trends and cultural shifts on TikTok.
- Algorithm Changes: Adapt your strategies in response to algorithm changes and updates.
- Community Feedback: Listen to audience feedback and adjust strategies based on community preferences.

As we conclude our exploration of adjusting strategies based on TikTok Analytics, remember that data is a dynamic force that propels your content forward. In the subsequent sections of Chapter 7, we'll continue to unravel the intricacies of analyzing analytics, exploring strategies for leveraging data-driven insights, optimizing collaborations, and additional elements that contribute to TikTok mastery. Get ready to refine your dance with data, respond to the rhythms of audience engagement, and elevate your TikTok performance to new heights.

Chapter 8: Going Beyond Virality

Welcome to the concluding chapter of "Mastering TikTok: A Guide to Creating Viral Videos." As we reach the culmination of this transformative journey through the realms of creativity, strategy, and community, Chapter 8 beckons us to explore a dimension that transcends the allure of viral fame. Aptly titled "Going Beyond Virality," this chapter invites you to reflect on the enduring impact of your TikTok presence and how it can extend far beyond the metrics of likes and shares.

Virality is a thrilling aspect of TikTok success, but this chapter challenges you to consider what happens after the viral moment subsides. It's an exploration of sustainability, influence, and the legacy you wish to leave within the TikTok community. As we navigate this chapter, we'll delve into strategies for maintaining relevance, building a lasting brand, and evolving as a creator in the ever-changing landscape of social media.

Discover the significance of authenticity as a driving force for enduring connections with your audience. We'll explore the role of consistency not only in content creation but in cultivating a genuine relationship with your followers. Additionally, we'll discuss how to navigate challenges, setbacks, and even the inevitable shifts in trends that accompany the evolving nature of digital platforms.

This chapter is an invitation to think beyond the immediate and embrace the journey of continuous growth as a TikTok creator. We'll delve into strategies for diversifying your content, exploring new avenues, and positioning yourself as a thought leader within your niche.

Whether you're a TikTok sensation or an emerging creator, Chapter 8 serves as a compass for navigating the complexities of sustained success. Let's embark on this final leg of our journey, exploring the profound impact your presence can have within the TikTok community and beyond. Get ready to go beyond virality, leaving an indelible mark as you master the art of TikTok and shape the narrative of your digital legacy.

8.1 Monetization Strategies

As you navigate the vibrant landscape of TikTok, transcending virality opens the door to a world of possibilities, including the potential to turn your passion into a sustainable endeavor. Welcome to Chapter 8 of "Mastering TikTok: A Guide to Creating Viral Videos," where we explore monetization strategies—an exciting chapter that unveils the pathways to transforming your TikTok presence into a source of income.

The Evolution of TikTok Monetization

TikTok has evolved beyond being solely a platform for creative expression; it has become a space where creators can leverage their influence and content creation skills for financial gain. TikTok's monetization features offer opportunities to earn money directly from your content and engage with your audience in new and impactful ways.

1. TikTok Creator Fund

The TikTok Creator Fund is a groundbreaking initiative that allows eligible creators to earn money directly from TikTok. To qualify, creators need to meet certain criteria, including:

- Age Requirement: Creators must be at least 18 years old.
- Follower Count: A minimum of 100,000 followers.
- Video Views: A minimum of 100,000 video views in the last 30 days.

Once accepted into the Creator Fund, creators can earn money based on a variety of factors, including video engagement and views. This provides a steady stream of income for creators who meet the eligibility requirements.

Tips for Success:
- Consistent Quality Content: Maintain a consistent schedule of high-quality content to engage your audience and boost your chances of meeting eligibility criteria.
- Audience Engagement: Foster engagement through comments, likes, and shares to enhance your overall video views and increase your chances of qualifying.

2. Live Gifts and Virtual Items

TikTok Live allows you to connect with your audience in real-time, and with the ability to receive gifts from viewers, creators can earn monetary rewards. Viewers can purchase virtual gifts using TikTok Coins and send them to creators during live broadcasts. Creators receive a portion of the value of the gifts as a form of monetization.

Tips for Success:
- Interactive Live Sessions: Plan interactive and engaging live sessions to encourage viewer participation and gift-giving.
- Express Gratitude: Acknowledge and thank viewers for their gifts during live broadcasts to foster a positive and supportive community.

3. Brand Partnerships and Sponsorships

Collaborating with brands and securing sponsorships is a potent avenue for monetization on TikTok. As your influence grows, brands may approach you for partnerships, or you can actively seek out collaborations that align with your content and audience.

Tips for Success:
- Authentic Alignments: Choose brands and partnerships that align authentically with your content and resonate with your audience.
- Transparency: Clearly communicate any sponsored content to maintain transparency and trust with your followers.
- Negotiate Fairly: Establish fair compensation for your collaborations, considering factors such as reach, engagement, and exclusivity.

4. Selling Merchandise

TikTok's Merch Shelf feature allows eligible creators to showcase and sell their merchandise directly on their TikTok profiles. This integrated approach enables creators to leverage their TikTok platform to promote and sell products, expanding revenue streams beyond content monetization.

Tips for Success:
- Branded Merchandise: Design merchandise that reflects your brand and resonates with your audience.
- Promotion through Content: Feature your merchandise in your videos and use creative content to promote and drive sales.
- Quality and Transparency: Ensure the quality of your merchandise and maintain transparency with your audience regarding product details.

5. Offering Premium Content

TikTok is exploring the concept of offering premium content subscriptions, allowing creators to provide exclusive content to subscribers for a recurring fee. While this feature is in its early stages, it presents an additional avenue for creators to monetize their unique content and offer special perks to dedicated followers.

Tips for Success:

- Unique Value Proposition: Provide exclusive content that offers unique value to subscribers.
- Engagement and Interactivity: Foster a sense of community and engagement among subscribers with exclusive interactions and behind-the-scenes content.
- Pricing Strategy: Set subscription fees that reflect the value of the premium content and align with audience expectations.

As we conclude our exploration of monetization strategies on TikTok, remember that the journey beyond virality is a multifaceted adventure. Each monetization avenue offers unique opportunities to transform your creative passion into a sustainable endeavor. In the subsequent sections of Chapter 8, we'll continue to unravel the intricacies of going beyond virality, exploring strategies for building a personal brand, cultivating a loyal community, and additional elements that contribute to TikTok mastery. Get ready to embark on a transformative journey as you navigate the exciting landscape of TikTok monetization.

8.2 Building a Brand on TikTok

In the ever-evolving world of TikTok, transcending virality is not just about fleeting fame—it's about building a lasting presence that resonates with your audience. Welcome to Chapter 8 of "Mastering TikTok: A Guide to Creating Viral Videos," where we explore the art of building a brand on TikTok—an indispensable chapter that goes beyond the numbers, focusing on cultivating a meaningful connection with your audience and establishing a brand that stands the test of time.

The Essence of Brand Building on TikTok

Building a brand on TikTok is more than creating entertaining videos; it's about crafting a distinctive identity that encapsulates your values, personality, and the unique essence of your content. As you embark on this journey, consider the following strategies to solidify your brand presence on TikTok:

1. Define Your Brand Identity

Clarity of Purpose:
Clearly define the purpose and mission of your brand. Whether it's entertainment, education, or a unique blend of both, a clear sense of purpose forms the foundation of your brand identity.

Values and Voice:
Identify the core values that guide your content creation. Develop a consistent and authentic voice that aligns with these values, resonating with your audience on a deeper level.

Visual Branding:
Craft a visual identity that sets your brand apart. This includes elements such as your profile picture, video aesthetics, and any consistent visual themes that become synonymous with your brand.

2. Consistency in Content

Theme and Niche:
Maintain a consistent theme or niche that defines your content. Whether it's comedy, beauty, education, or a unique combination, consistency reinforces your brand message and attracts a dedicated audience.

Content Quality:

Prioritize the quality of your content. Strive for excellence in production, storytelling, and engagement. Consistent high-quality content reinforces your brand's credibility and encourages audience loyalty.

Posting Schedule:
Establish a consistent posting schedule. Regular and predictable content updates create anticipation among your audience, fostering a habit of returning to your profile for fresh content.

3. Audience Engagement

Community Interaction:
Engage with your audience authentically. Respond to comments, acknowledge your followers, and actively participate in the community. Building a sense of community around your brand enhances audience connection.

Collaborations:
Collaborate with other creators strategically. Choose collaborations that align with your brand values and introduce your content to new audiences. Collaborations contribute to a dynamic brand narrative.

Feedback Integration:
Listen to audience feedback and integrate it into your content strategy. Understanding your audience's preferences and concerns enables you to evolve your brand in response to their needs.

4. Leveraging TikTok Features

Utilize Features Creatively:
Explore and leverage TikTok's features creatively. Whether it's filters, effects, duets, or stitches, use these features to enhance your storytelling and create a unique brand signature.

Participate in Challenges:
Actively participate in TikTok challenges. Aligning with trending challenges not only keeps your content fresh but also positions your brand within the larger TikTok culture.

Live Interaction:
Engage with your audience through TikTok Live. Live sessions provide an opportunity for real-time interaction, Q&A sessions, and fostering a closer connection with your followers.

5. Showcase Behind-the-Scenes

Authenticity and Transparency:
Offer glimpses behind the scenes of your content creation process. Authenticity and transparency build trust with your audience, allowing them to connect with the person behind the content.

Personal Stories:
Share personal stories that align with your brand narrative. Whether it's challenges, successes, or lessons learned, weaving personal anecdotes into your content humanizes your brand.

Day in the Life:
Consider showcasing a "day in the life" to give your audience a more comprehensive view of your world. This can include aspects of your daily routine, creative process, or interactions with the TikTok

community.

6. Utilize TikTok Analytics

Data-Driven Decision Making:
Leverage TikTok Analytics to gain insights into your audience, content performance, and trends. Use data-driven insights to refine your content strategy, optimize posting times, and align with audience preferences.

Monitor Growth:
Regularly monitor your growth metrics, including follower count, video views, and engagement. Understand what contributes to growth and adapt your strategies to sustain and amplify this momentum.

Refine Strategies:
Adjust your brand-building strategies based on analytics data. Identify top-performing content, refine posting schedules, and adapt to evolving audience behaviors to ensure your brand remains relevant.

7. Establish Cross-Platform Presence

Multi-Platform Approach:
Extend your brand beyond TikTok by establishing a presence on other social media platforms. Cross-promote your TikTok content on platforms like Instagram, YouTube, or Twitter to broaden your audience reach.

Consistent Branding:
Maintain consistent branding across platforms. This includes profile pictures, visual aesthetics, and messaging. Consistent branding reinforces your brand identity and facilitates seamless cross-platform recognition.

Diversify Content:

Tailor your content for each platform while maintaining a cohesive brand narrative. Diversifying content ensures that your brand remains adaptable to the unique dynamics of each platform.

As we conclude our exploration of building a brand on TikTok, remember that the essence of brand building lies in the authenticity of your connection with the audience. In the subsequent sections of Chapter 8, we'll continue to unravel the intricacies of going beyond virality, exploring strategies for cultivating a loyal community, optimizing collaborations, and additional elements that contribute to TikTok mastery. Get ready to embark on a transformative journey of brand evolution as you navigate the dynamic landscape of TikTok.

Conclusion and Recap of Key Strategies

Congratulations on completing "Mastering TikTok: A Guide to Creating Viral Videos." This journey has been a comprehensive exploration of the art, science, and community that define success on

TikTok. As we conclude this guide, let's recap the key strategies that can empower you to not only create viral videos but to thrive as a thoughtful and influential TikTok creator.

1. Crafting Captivating Content (Chapter 2): Your content is the heart of your TikTok journey. We've explored the elements that make videos stand out, from storytelling techniques to understanding the pulse of TikTok trends. Remember, your creativity is the key to capturing and retaining the attention of your audience.

2. Optimizing Your Profile (Chapter 3): Your profile is your digital identity. We discussed the importance of a compelling profile picture, a captivating bio, and the strategic use of links and hashtags. A well-optimized profile is your invitation to potential followers, providing a snapshot of what makes your TikTok presence unique.

3. Leveraging TikTok Features (Chapter 4): TikTok offers a plethora of features to enhance your content. From duets and challenges to filters and effects, we've explored how to use these tools creatively. Mastering these features expands your creative toolkit and can set your content apart in a sea of videos.

4. Consistency and Timing (Chapter 5): In Chapter 5, we emphasized the importance of consistency in your posting schedule and thematic elements. Timing your posts strategically, aligning with trends, and staying attuned to cultural events enhance your visibility and engagement on TikTok.

5. Engaging with the TikTok Community (Chapter 6): Chapter 6 focused on the vibrant TikTok community. Engaging with your audience through comments, duets, and challenges builds a sense of connection. Being authentic and participating in the communal spirit of TikTok can turn viewers into dedicated followers.

6. Analyzing Analytics (Chapter 7): In Chapter 7, we delved into the world of analytics. Understanding your performance metrics is key to refining your content strategy. TikTok analytics provide valuable insights into audience demographics, watch time, and engagement, helping you make informed decisions for sustainable growth.

7. Going Beyond Virality (Chapter 8): As we concluded in Chapter 8, going beyond virality involves sustaining your impact. Authenticity, consistency, and adaptability are crucial as you navigate the evolving landscape of TikTok. This chapter encouraged you to consider the lasting legacy you want to leave within the TikTok community.

Remember, mastering TikTok is an ongoing journey. Stay curious, keep experimenting, and embrace the evolution of your content. Whether you're an emerging creator or a seasoned TikTok enthusiast, the strategies outlined in this guide provide a foundation for success. Thank you for joining us on this adventure, and may your TikTok journey be filled with creativity, connection, and continuous growth. Happy creating!

8.2 Building a Brand on TikTok

In the ever-evolving world of TikTok, transcending virality is not just about fleeting fame—it's about building a lasting presence that resonates with your audience. Welcome to Chapter 8 of "Mastering

TikTok: A Guide to Creating Viral Videos," where we explore the art of building a brand on TikTok—an indispensable chapter that goes beyond the numbers, focusing on cultivating a meaningful connection with your audience and establishing a brand that stands the test of time.

The Essence of Brand Building on TikTok

Building a brand on TikTok is more than creating entertaining videos; it's about crafting a distinctive identity that encapsulates your values, personality, and the unique essence of your content. As you embark on this journey, consider the following strategies to solidify your brand presence on TikTok:

1. Define Your Brand Identity

Clarity of Purpose:
Clearly define the purpose and mission of your brand. Whether it's entertainment, education, or a unique blend of both, a clear sense of purpose forms the foundation of your brand identity.

Values and Voice:
Identify the core values that guide your content creation. Develop a consistent and authentic voice that aligns with these values, resonating with your audience on a deeper level.

Visual Branding:
Craft a visual identity that sets your brand apart. This includes elements such as your profile picture, video aesthetics, and any consistent visual themes that become synonymous with your brand.

2. Consistency in Content

Theme and Niche:
Maintain a consistent theme or niche that defines your content. Whether it's comedy, beauty, education, or a unique combination, consistency reinforces your brand message and attracts a dedicated audience.

Content Quality:
Prioritize the quality of your content. Strive for excellence in production, storytelling, and engagement. Consistent high-quality content reinforces your brand's credibility and encourages audience loyalty.

Posting Schedule:
Establish a consistent posting schedule. Regular and predictable content updates create anticipation among your audience, fostering a habit of returning to your profile for fresh content.

3. Audience Engagement

Community Interaction:
Engage with your audience authentically. Respond to comments, acknowledge your followers, and actively participate in the community. Building a sense of community around your brand enhances audience connection.

Collaborations:
Collaborate with other creators strategically. Choose collaborations that align with your brand values and introduce your content to new audiences. Collaborations contribute to a dynamic brand narrative.

Feedback Integration:
Listen to audience feedback and integrate it into your content strategy. Understanding your audience's preferences and concerns enables you to evolve your brand in response to their needs.

4. Leveraging TikTok Features

Utilize Features Creatively:
Explore and leverage TikTok's features creatively. Whether it's filters, effects, duets, or stitches, use these features to enhance your storytelling and create a unique brand signature.

Participate in Challenges:
Actively participate in TikTok challenges. Aligning with trending challenges not only keeps your content fresh but also positions your brand within the larger TikTok culture.

Live Interaction:
Engage with your audience through TikTok Live. Live sessions provide an opportunity for real-time interaction, Q&A sessions, and fostering a closer connection with your followers.

5. Showcase Behind-the-Scenes

Authenticity and Transparency:
Offer glimpses behind the scenes of your content creation process. Authenticity and transparency build trust with your audience, allowing them to connect with the person behind the content.

Personal Stories:
Share personal stories that align with your brand narrative. Whether it's challenges, successes, or lessons learned, weaving personal anecdotes into your content humanizes your brand.

Day in the Life:
Consider showcasing a "day in the life" to give your audience a more comprehensive view of your world. This can include aspects of your daily routine, creative process, or interactions with the TikTok community.

6. Utilize TikTok Analytics

Data-Driven Decision Making:
Leverage TikTok Analytics to gain insights into your audience, content performance, and trends. Use data-driven insights to refine your content strategy, optimize posting times, and align with audience preferences.

Monitor Growth:
Regularly monitor your growth metrics, including follower count, video views, and engagement. Understand what contributes to growth and adapt your strategies to sustain and amplify this momentum.

Refine Strategies:
Adjust your brand-building strategies based on analytics data. Identify top-performing content, refine posting schedules, and adapt to evolving audience behaviors to ensure your brand remains relevant.

7. Establish Cross-Platform Presence

Multi-Platform Approach:
Extend your brand beyond TikTok by establishing a presence on other social media platforms. Cross-promote your TikTok content on platforms like Instagram, YouTube, or Twitter to broaden your audience reach.

Consistent Branding:
Maintain consistent branding across platforms. This includes profile pictures, visual aesthetics, and messaging. Consistent branding reinforces your brand identity and facilitates seamless cross-platform recognition.

Diversify Content:

Tailor your content for each platform while maintaining a cohesive brand narrative. Diversifying content ensures that your brand remains adaptable to the unique dynamics of each platform.

As we conclude our exploration of building a brand on TikTok, remember that the essence of brand building lies in the authenticity of your connection with the audience. In the subsequent sections of Chapter 8, we'll continue to unravel the intricacies of going beyond virality, exploring strategies for cultivating a loyal community, optimizing collaborations, and additional elements that contribute to TikTok mastery. Get ready to embark on a transformative journey of brand evolution as you navigate the dynamic landscape of TikTok.

BONUS TOOLS

Mastering TikTok involves not only creating compelling content but also leveraging third-party tools to enhance your strategy, analytics, and overall experience on the platform. Here are some popular third-party tools for TikTok, along with brief descriptions of their features:

1. Inflact's TikTok Downloader:
   - Purpose: Inflact's TikTok Downloader allows you to download TikTok videos without the TikTok watermark.
   - Key Features:
     - Download videos in high quality.
     - No watermark on downloaded videos.
     - Simple and user-friendly interface.

2. TokUpgrade:
   - Purpose: TokUpgrade is a growth service designed to increase your TikTok followers organically.
   - Key Features:
     - Targeted growth based on your niche and preferences.
     - Real and engaged followers.
     - Smart targeting to reach your ideal audience.

3. TikTok Analytics Tools:
   - Purpose: Various third-party analytics tools provide in-depth insights into your TikTok account's performance.

- Key Features:
  - Detailed analytics on followers, views, engagement, and growth.
  - Track popular trends and hashtags.
  - Understand the demographics of your audience.

4. Clipchamp:
   - Purpose: Clipchamp is a video editing tool that can help you create engaging TikTok content with professional-quality edits.
   - Key Features:
     - User-friendly video editing interface.
     - Add filters, transitions, and text to your videos.
     - Create and edit videos directly in your browser.

5. Tokboard:
   - Purpose: Tokboard is a TikTok analytics tool that provides insights into TikTok profiles and content.
   - Key Features:
     - Track follower growth and engagement.
     - Analyze top-performing content and hashtags.
     - Compare your performance with other TikTok profiles.

6. TikTok Money Calculator:
   - Purpose: This tool estimates potential earnings for TikTok creators based on their follower count and engagement.
   - Key Features:
     - Estimate earnings per post based on engagement metrics.
     - Understand the potential monetary value of your TikTok presence.

7. Tik Analytics:
   - Purpose: Tik Analytics is an app that provides detailed analytics for TikTok creators.
   - Key Features:
     - Track follower growth and engagement trends.
     - Analyze video performance and audience demographics.
     - Receive insights to optimize your content strategy.

8. VidNice:
   - Purpose: VidNice is a video downloader and watermark remover for TikTok.
   - Key Features:
     - Download TikTok videos without a watermark.
     - Save videos in high resolution.
     - User-friendly interface for easy downloads.

9. Tiklytics:
   - Purpose: Tiklytics is a comprehensive analytics platform specifically designed for TikTok creators.
   - Key Features:
     - Track follower growth, video views, and engagement.
     - Identify popular hashtags and trends.
     - Receive recommendations for content optimization.

10. TikTok Fonts Generator:

- Purpose: Spice up your TikTok captions and bio with unique fonts using a TikTok Fonts Generator.
- Key Features:
  - Convert your text into various creative fonts.
  - Enhance the visual appeal of your captions and bio.

Before using any third-party tools, it's essential to ensure their credibility and adherence to TikTok's terms of service to avoid potential issues with your account. Always prioritize tools that add value to your TikTok experience and contribute positively to your content strategy and growth.

Unleashing Creativity with CapCut

CapCut, a versatile and user-friendly video editing app, is your secret weapon in the quest for TikTok virality. In this chapter of "Mastering TikTok: A Guide to Creating Viral Videos," we delve into the power of CapCut, unlocking its features to elevate your content creation game and increase your chances of going viral.

Understanding CapCut: A Brief Overview

CapCut, developed by Bytedance (the same company behind TikTok), is a comprehensive video editing tool that empowers creators with a plethora of features. Whether you're a seasoned video editor or just starting on your TikTok journey, CapCut provides a seamless and intuitive platform to enhance your videos.

Why CapCut?

1. Intuitive Interface:
   - CapCut boasts a user-friendly interface, making it accessible for beginners while offering advanced features for experienced creators.

2. Feature-Rich Editing:
   - From basic cuts and trims to advanced transitions, filters, and effects, CapCut provides a comprehensive suite of editing tools.

3. Music and Sound Effects:
   - Access a vast library of royalty-free music and sound effects to enhance the audio quality of your videos.

4. Rich Library of Effects:
   - Explore a variety of effects, including filters, stickers, and animations, to add flair and creativity to your content.

5. Professional Touch:
   - CapCut allows for precise editing, enabling you to add a professional touch to your videos without the need for complex software.

CapCut for Viral Success: Tips and Tricks

1. Engaging Introductions:
   - Capture your audience's attention from the start. Use CapCut's editing features to create dynamic

and visually appealing introductions.

2. Seamless Transitions:
   - Smooth transitions between scenes keep viewers hooked. Experiment with CapCut's transition effects to add a polished touch to your videos.

3. Creative Filters and Effects:
   - Stand out with creative filters and effects. CapCut offers a diverse range of options to enhance the visual appeal of your content.

4. Dynamic Text Overlays:
   - Use dynamic text overlays to convey messages or highlight key points. CapCut's text editing features allow for customization and creativity.

5. Optimized Video Speed:
   - Experiment with video speed adjustments to create dramatic or comedic effects. CapCut's speed control feature lets you play with the tempo of your content.

6. Incorporate Trending Sounds:
   - Stay on trend by incorporating popular sounds and music. CapCut's extensive audio library ensures you have a wide selection to choose from.

7. Storytelling Sequences:
   - Tell a compelling story through your videos. CapCut's editing capabilities enable you to arrange clips in a narrative sequence, keeping your audience engaged.

8. Enhanced Color Grading:
   - Experiment with color grading to enhance the visual aesthetics of your videos. CapCut allows for precise adjustments to achieve the desired look.

9. Diverse Aspect Ratios:
   - Optimize your videos for different platforms by utilizing CapCut's support for various aspect ratios. This flexibility ensures your content looks great across different social media channels.

10. Watermark Removal:
    - While creating content on CapCut, ensure a clean and professional look by utilizing its feature to remove watermarks.

CapCut and TikTok Integration:

CapCut seamlessly integrates with TikTok, allowing for a smooth transition from editing to publishing. Follow these steps to maximize the synergy between CapCut and TikTok:

1. Edit in CapCut:
   - Craft and refine your videos in CapCut, leveraging its extensive editing features.

2. Export in TikTok-Compatible Format:
   - Ensure your edited video is exported in a format compatible with TikTok's upload requirements.

3. Upload Directly to TikTok:
   - Utilize CapCut's integration with TikTok to upload your edited videos directly to the platform.

4. Leverage Hashtags and Captions:
   - Craft attention-grabbing captions and use relevant hashtags on TikTok to enhance the discoverability of your content.

CapCut serves as a dynamic companion on your journey to TikTok mastery. Whether you're aiming for viral fame or simply looking to enhance your creative expression, the powerful editing capabilities of CapCut empower you to stand out in the crowded TikTok landscape. Experiment, innovate, and let your creativity shine as you harness the full potential of CapCut on your quest to TikTok stardom.